NOT YOUR ORDINARY BOOK.

The bookstores are filled with books claiming to help you succeed in your small business. Some of them are good. Most are not.

Why?

Many are written by authors who have never succeeded in a business of their own. Their books are based on a textbook approach to managing a business.

In your hands you hold a book written by one of the leading resources in America on Small Business Success.

The wisdom, insights, strategies, and ideas revealed in this book are proven in the real world every day.

ABOUT MARK LEBLANC

Mark LeBlanc has been self-employed virtually his entire adult life. With deep commitment and quiet confidence, he has devoted his life to helping others create an innerpreneurial mindset and creating a life of possibilities.

In 1997, The Minnesota Speakers Association created *The Mark LeBlanc Award For Outstanding Service* and presents this award annually to a deserving member.

He currently lives in La Jolla, CA with Jill. They have been married for more than 14 years. Mark loves to walk, eat, nap, watch movies, and spend time with his family, friends, and colleagues.

FINALLY, A BOOK ABOUT GROWING A
BUSINESS THAT MAKES SENSE!

GROWING
YOUR
BUSINESS!

What You Need To Know
What You Need To Do

MARK LEBLANC

Foreword by
Tom Winninger, CSP, CPAE

Beaver's Pond Press

Edina, Minnesota

ISBN: 1-890676-38-1

Library of Congress Catalog Number: 99-63182

Creative Work by Mori Studio
Illustrations by Jody Winger
Editorial Assistance by Mary Coons

First Printing: October, 1999
Printed in the United States of America.

04   03   02   01   00   99   8 7 6 5 4 3 2 1

For information contact:

Beaver's Pond Press

5125 Danen's Drive
Edina, Minnesota 55439-1465
(612) 829-8818

For Ralph & Lois LeBlanc

*who by example, taught me more
of business and life than they
could possibly know*

I love you.

Contents

FOREWORD
by Tom Winninger, CSP, CPAE

My life's work has taken me around the world. I've met literally thousands of people, many of whom I find to be compelling and infinitely interesting, yet only a handful come to mind when I think of those who have deeply impacted and changed my life both personally and professionally. One such person is Mark LeBlanc.

I first met Mark in 1983 at a convention for the National Speakers Association. It was easy to see that he possessed a unique combination of enthusiasm, desire, and talent that would serve to create a benchmark for others to model. I knew then he would be a driving force in the marketplace.

However the real defining moment for me came in 1996 when I went to Mark for consultation with him regarding my own business. The outcome of that first meeting can be stated no more clearly than to say my business has doubled since then. That increase is directly connected to the focus he brings to the process of true growth. Because of his pure strategy process I was able to redefine my business, allowing me to capture and hold my customers' attention.

Growing Your Business! will help you do just that. In it, Mark has provided many insights and tools that are anchored to his true growth strategies. The results of reading and putting this book into action will impact your business as well as your personal life. It is an agent for change today and a bridge to your future success.

Tom Winninger, CSP, CPAE

Author of *Price Wars, Full Price,* and *Sell Easy*

CEO, The Winninger Institute

INTRODUCTION

"I'm not sure you can make it on your own. I don't think you have the work ethic to run your own business."

Richard Gossen
Milaca, Minnesota
December, 1982

Those words still ring in my mind. I was 21 years old. I am sure he was trying to make some kind of point.

Six months later, I was self-employed. After ten years of running my own creative and printing company, I started Small Business Success.

Anyone can start a business.

It is staying in business and growing it that causes so much angst and heartache in the small business world. Hopefully, this simple book will provide a piece of advice, a strategy, and a little bit of encouragement.

Mark LeBlanc
Small Business Success

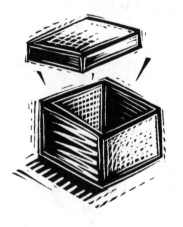

The box or model provides a framework for your business.

1

CREATE A MODEL
THAT DRIVES YOU!

For years I have heard experts promote the concept of being creative. You must think outside the box. Be creative.

I must admit I would nod and agree. Yet, I did not comprehend what they were saying. One day it dawned on me the reason most people cannot think outside the box is the simple fact they don't have a box to begin with.

It's as if a person went to an office supply store and purchased one of those flat bankers-type boxes or storage boxes, brought it home, and tried to assemble it.

Even though the instructions are printed right on the box, you're flipping and twisting, tossing, and cursing; and then somehow by magic it comes together, and you begin to use it.

My objective is to help you create a box for your business or professional practice. I refer to putting the box together as an example of putting together the right model for your business. Your model should do two things.

You can run your business, make money, and have fun doing it!

It should:

• drive you. You can get excited about it.

• be a model that others fit into.

Greater Likelihood

If you put together the right model for your business, you will have a greater likelihood that your fun meter will be on maximum and your stress meter will be on minimum.

After a number of years, I know that owning and operating your own business can be fun. The sooner you realize this, the better off you will be.

Remember Forrest Gump?

In the opening scenes of the hit movie *Forrest Gump*, the scenery is beautiful, the music is soothing, and you notice a feather floating carelessly and freely wherever the wind takes it.

Danger! Many small businesses are like that feather. You go where the wind takes you, where your employees lead you, and your customers dare you.

Spontaneity is positive. Only I would rather see spontaneity occur within a defined framework for your business. Without a framework in place, you can grow, though it could be stressful and chaotic.

Others Fit In

By "Others," I mean other people, projects, products, prospects, customers, employees, suppliers, etc.

If they fit into your model, and your way of being in business and your way of doing business, you will have more fun.

Running your own business can be stressful enough the way it is. Statistics come out every so often by the Small Business Administration and other organizations. They trumpet the idea that five out of ten businesses fail within one year, and that nine out of ten will not make it to their fifth business anniversary.

Most people think it is due to lack of capital or losing to the competition. It's not. It is due to a lack of courage and a lack of creativity. This leads to a lack of customers.

Read the stories of any of the great entrepreneurs over the years, and you will find success in the midst of great adversity. Or simply ask anyone around you who has been in business for five or more years. Most will tell you the same thing I am going to share with you right now. So few people will ever do what it takes to make things happen in their own business and life. Will you?

Simple, But Not Basic

I conducted a Growing Your Business presentation in Denver, Colorado, and a gentleman in the audience by the name of Scott Halford was most enthusiastic. Following the presentation, he remarked that my program was one of simplicity and yet it was not basic.

After thinking about it, I realized that one of the reasons it was not basic was the difficulty in achieving that level of simplicity.

When you see something in the marketplace that seems so ordinary and simple, it usually is the culmination of sweat, blood, and tears. Enormous amounts of time, energy, money, and creativity are required to produce a product or campaign that works. Then a product or service finds its way into the hearts, minds, and souls of people in the marketplace.

Your Model

In this book, I will focus more on the direction you want to go, and what I believe it will take for you to get there. Much of the content, material, exercises, and ideas will be focused on growth concepts and strategies.

Along the way, I will provide you with several new perspectives or variations on ideas that exist in the business world today. If you feel a certain amount of resistance to a concept, a strategy, or an idea, then ask yourself a simple question.

What is the greater likelihood that this idea might work for me versus the same old way I have been approaching this in my business?

Most of the stress in business is self-imposed. It can result from setting unrealistic goals with no model in place. This can lead to sleepless nights, poor cash flow, wrong decisions, employee turnover, divorce, early death, and on and on.

If you set goals within the framework of a model, you will be on the right track. When I am feeling stressed, I will step back and evaluate what is causing it. Invariably, I discover I have deviated from my model and am working on the wrong project, with the wrong customer, using the wrong product, or with the wrong supplier or vendor.

When I make the decisions that bring me back to my model, the stress melts away and I can get back to having fun in my business. Sometimes it happens so fast, it seems like magic.

Your model is comprised of many things, and the following five areas will help you create one for your business. We'll address a few of these areas and the rest will be up to you. Your model will evolve and grow over time.

This is your opportunity to gaze into a crystal ball and imagine what an ideal business would look like and feel like.

*There are no unrealistic goals,
only unrealistic timeframes.*

*However, it can happen sooner
rather than later!*

1. Business Planning

I run my business:

_____   a.)   with a to-do list and no plan.

_____   b.)   with a plan that contains a
            to-do list.

_____   c.)   in my head.

The most successful businesses are those that have some type of written plan. Plans can come in a variety of forms. It doesn't matter if you have a short or long plan, a simple or complex plan; but, it makes good sense to have a plan.

People say they don't want a plan because they don't need to borrow any money from outside sources. A plan is more for you than a bank. A written plan provides you with a sense of direction, and will help you make better decisions. The best plans provide a solid overview of your business and what you want to see happen in the next five years, the next three years, the next 12 months, the next three months, and the next 30 days.

Out of that plan you can develop a to-do list that will keep you focused and on track. With no plan in place, it is easy to go off on tangents disguised as opportunities. There is power in a well-written, narrative plan. For some of you, an executive summary is all you need. An executive summary is a short three to ten page overview or introduction to a more formal plan.

 From The Idea File

1. Write an executive summary.

You can get an outline from a book on business planning or purchase a software program that contains examples or language and templates; i.e., BizPlan Builder by Jian Software Company.

2. Carry your executive summary with you.

When you are finished, three hole punch your plan, and put it in your day planner or weekly schedule.

3. Evaluate your plan on a regular basis.

Spend one hour each month evaluating and updating your plan. You can add and delete where necessary. Over time it will become a powerful, working document.

2. Financial Management

From a financial perspective, answer the following questions. In an ideal month, your business would reach the numbers listed below.

Our gross revenues* would be $_____.

My compensation would be $_____.

Gross revenues will be referred to as an optimistic number later on in this book.

Stop! Do not read further until you answer these questions. Some of you will be tempted to move on. Please, do not. Some of you will wonder if I want your answers for some month down the road when things are going well. I don't.

Look into your crystal ball and answer the questions for right now. Don't allow your mind to set limits for you. You are in control of your business, and now is the time to take charge. If you don't, your prospects will be in charge, or your customers will be in charge, or your suppliers will be in charge, or your employees will be in charge. These are the wrong people to put in charge.

a.m.

What am I doing today to reach my optimistic number?

p.m.

What did I do today to reach my optimistic number?

There are no unrealistic goals, only
unrealistic time frames.

This expression is used as a form of comfort for people who do not reach their goals and get what they want when they want it.

You can reach your goals sooner rather than later if you are focused. The challenge you face is creating a laser-like focus. If you are clear about how much you want and what you are willing to do for it, you can make things happen sooner rather than later.

 **From
The
Idea
File**

1.   Identify your optimistic number.*

$ _____

Your optimistic number is your gross revenues deposited on a monthly basis.

2.   Ask yourself the a.m./p.m. questions.

For the next 30 days I want you to ask yourself two questions. In the morning, your a.m. question is:

What am I doing today to reach my optimistic number?

At the end of the day, your p.m. question is:

What did I do today to reach my optimistic number?

3. Write your optimistic number on a Post-it™ note and put it in your daily planner. It will serve as a reminder of what you want.

4. Evaluate your optimistic number every 90 days. Over time you may increase or decrease your number with respect to the decisions you make in your business.

5. Put financial pros on your team.

It is vital you work with a bookkeeping service or accountant and maybe both. In addition, you may want an insurance agent, financial planner, and a payroll service.

You are never too small to surround yourself with the right resources that will ensure a strong foundation for your business.

3. Selling Strategies

Everyone sells! Selling is the key to your success. If you are unable to sell your products and services to a prospect, you will go nowhere except to the graveyard of entrepreneurs and business owners.

It is the critical skill that will determine what you deposit and how it affects your bottom line. Seldom does any product or service sell itself.

The good news is that selling is nothing more than a communication process. When you are able to speak or visit with a prospect and share your story, good things happen.

 From The Idea File

1. Brainstorm and develop the answers to the following core questions:

    a.) What do you do?

    b.) How do you do it?

    c.) Why should someone buy from you?

    d.) What can your customers expect?

    e.) What do you charge?

2.   Find a partner and role play.

Practice makes perfect and provides you with confidence. Prospects prefer to buy from a business person that exudes confidence, not hesitancy.

3.   Buy a book on selling.

> Recommendation:
> *The Greatest Salesman In The World*
> by Og Mandino

4. Marketing, Advertising, and Promotion

In the small business world, our revenues tend to reflect the path of a roller coaster. Up and down, up and down. One of the reasons for that scenario is the sporadic efforts we make when we market, advertise, and promote our products and services.

We market, market, market, sell, sell, sell, and deliver, deliver, deliver. Strike a balance between a marketing project versus a program.

A project is defined as a single initiative with an anticipated short-term result. Sometimes they work and sometimes they don't. A program is defined as an ongoing initiative with anticipated results over time.

Examples of Projects

- create a brochure
- mail 1,000 direct mail pieces
- update database
- place an ad in the newspaper

Examples of Programs

- develop a quarterly newsletter program
- mail 250 direct mail pieces each month
- spend $750 on display ads each quarter
- exhibit at two trade shows each year

 From The Idea File

1. Create an identity.

Hire a creative resource who will help you design a visual identity that will support you in the marketplace. It is likely you will need a graphic designer, a writer/editor, and in some cases, a publicist or public relations professional. These are important members of your team.

2. Create a plan to get you more business.

Create a marketing, advertising, and promotional plan that contains a combination of projects and programs.

5. Human Resources

Human Resources is a term used in the big business world. Let's use it in the small business world. Even if you are a one person operation, the human side of your business is critical, as it is in the big business world.

Do you or will you have employees over time?

How do you intend to stay motivated?

Is your job description as an owner clear?

How much time off do you want and when?

Will you invest in education and training?

 **From The Idea File**

1.   Write your owner's job description.

Based on the effort you are giving your company, would you hire you?

2.   Plan your time off.

Look at your calendar and block out your vacation(s) and other time off over the next twelve months.

Four Commodities

You only have four commodities with respect to your business: time, energy, money, and creativity. Where are you willing to bet your time, your energy, your money, and your creativity where it has the greatest likelihood of helping you reach your optimistic number?

It is easy to get sidetracked and move away from creating what you want instead of what you think or what you need. You tend to get what you focus on.

Common Obstacles

Fear

Lack of Motivation

Level of Belief

No Money

Little Support

Family Obligations

Education

Focus

No Plan

2

POSITION YOURSELF
FOR MORE PROSPECTS

How you position yourself in the mind of your prospects and clients is critical to attracting more prospects and reaching the level of success you desire. You position yourself in many ways. Here are 10 for your consideration.

(not in any particular order)

1. Your appearance

2. The words you say

3. The tools you use

4. Your location

5. Your attitude

6. Your response time

7. The clothes you wear

8. The places you go

9. The people you connect with

10. The groups you belong to

**From
The
Idea
File**

1. Create a personal balance sheet.

Spend some time reflecting on your business and personal activities. It is difficult to separate the two when your personal identity can get so wrapped up in what you do for a living. Pay attention to the things that create a favorable impression in the marketplace.

The Greatest Single Obstacle

When you go to the marketplace, you are faced with a number of challenges, problems, and obstacles. One obstacle rises above the rest. It is:

> Your inability to communicate
> effectively what you do and who
> you do it with best.

Every day you are faced with the challenge of introducing yourself, picking up the telephone, writing copy for a brochure, ad, or sales letter, and in some form or fashion communicating to an individual or group what you do.

When you are unable to communicate clearly in the marketplace, it is easy to come up with all kinds of reasons for your lack of progress.

If you are unable to speak with any amount of intelligence, you will likely come face to face with an invisible shield out there in business land. You know exactly what I am referring to.

Every time you come in contact with a prospect or any person in the marketplace, you will have an invisible shield between you and the other person. How you communicate will determine if that shield comes down or it gets thicker.

If you are unaware the shield exists, you can take any indifference or rejection personally. It is your responsibility to position yourself and your firm in such a way that the shield comes down and you can have a meaningful conversation with another human being. Here is a strategy that will work:

> Position yourself by concept,
> instead of by your titles or your
> products and/or services.

There are three positioning strategies you can take in the marketplace. You can position yourself by your titles. You can position yourself by your products and/or your services. Or you can position yourself by concept and zero in on the outcomes of your work.

Positioning By Titles

Positioning with your titles is the most common strategy that people in business use. It is the focus on the hard-earned titles that you put on your business cards and usually the first words out of your mouth. Seldom are people attracted to your titles. Putting more than one title on your business card turns off more prospects.

Some examples would be:

doctor	realtor
printer	financial planner
consultant	speaker
banker	accountant
architect	engineer
chiropractor	hair stylist
designer	freelancer
stockbroker	plumber

and the list goes on.

Fifty percent of the marketplace will have a negative perception of your title. Most people have had a negative experience in the past with one of your competitors, or some public misperception has cast doubt on your profession as a whole. Some titles are worse than others.

Positioning By Products/Services

The second positioning strategy is positioning by your products and/or your services. Doing this can immediately put you right smack next to your competition.

Examples of products and services would be:

printing	accounting
real estate	insurance
dental	office furniture
legal services	estate planning
banking	cellular phones
computers	business planning
books	daycare
bicycles	cars
clothes	consulting

You can look in the Yellow Pages for hundreds and thousands more products and services.

If your primary efforts, introductions, and promotional materials are title-centered and product/service focused, then you must do anything you can to set yourself apart from your competition. Look at your tools and think about the last time you introduced yourself. How did you position yourself?

There is a third way and a better way.

Positioning By Concept

I understand your titles are hard-earned and our products and services are what we provide. But, my goal is to help you attract more prospects.

You can attract more prospects by moving to the third positioning strategy, that of positioning by concept. Another way to look at it, is to identify and focus on the outcomes of your work or what happens when customers use your products and services. That should be your primary strategy for differentiation in the marketplace.

What happens when someone uses your products and services, and are better for it? What are the outcomes of your stuff?

 From The Idea File

1. Make a list of the 10 primary outcomes of your company, products, and services.

If you identify the outcomes and then build your conversations, brochures, web site, packaging, etc. around these outcomes, you will attract more prospects. And more prospects leads to more sales.

2. Create a great defining statement.

A Defining Statement

The easiest way to position yourself by concept is to create a great defining statement. A defining statement is a simple answer to a simple question, "What do you do?"

When you can answer this simple question in a succinct and concise way that attracts more prospects, you will have reached a deeper level of connection with your prospects and customers.

It is not easy. In fact, it may be the hardest thing you will do in your business. However, the rewards are great. In fact, here is the best reason for creating a defining statement.

Whatever you charge for your products and/or services will most likely be perceived as an investment in the outcomes they provide versus a cost for satisfying a need or solving a problem.

How many times do you answer this question differently? Do your customers or even your family and friends really understand what you do? What if everyone knew? What if your employees could repeat your defining statement? Wow! Your business would be great!

On Ideas

When an idea can't be articulated simply, crisply, and accessibly, there is usually something wrong with it. When I hear a good idea, it has an effect on my mind and body. Sometimes I feel it in my stomach, other times in my throat, still others on my skin — a kind of instant truth detector test.

Michael Eisner
Disney

Personal Pain

When I started Small Business Success, I positioned myself by my titles; i.e., consultant, speaker, and business agent. No one was attracted to me in a way that he or she wanted to know more.

Frustrated, I then identified my five core areas of service. They were business planning, financial management, selling strategies, human resources and developing your M.A.P. (or marketing, advertising and promotion.) It was clear to me that most of the problems for small business owners fit neatly into one of these five areas of service. I went back to the marketplace and thought my business would surely take off and come to life.

Instead of attracting prospects, I repelled them. They ran away from me. I could not even give away my services. This was a painful period in my life.

With no progress, I went back to the drawing board and had another strategic planning meeting with myself. I asked myself a simple question, "What do you do?" My initial response was, "You are not doing anything. No one is interested in what you have to offer." I then asked myself another question that led me to a statement that changed my business forever.

Seven Rules For Creating A Defining Statement

1

Language

2

Conversational

3

Attraction

4

Dream Focus

5

Contains What And Who

6

Dual Focus

7

Repeatability

That question was, "What do you want to do?" I started to write, and here is what came out of that brainstorming meeting:

"I work with people who want to start a business and small business owners who want to grow their business."

I looked at this statement and thought it was too simple. But, I had nothing to lose and everything to gain. I went back to the marketplace and in 30 days seven prospects wrote me a check and engaged me in the process of helping them start or grow a small business.

At the time I didn't understand what happened. I just deposited the money and went to work on behalf of my clients. It took me more than two years to figure out I had gone beyond my titles and my services to the third positioning strategy. I now was focused on the outcomes of my work and what I had set out to do when I started my business. Today, I refer to this statement as a defining statement.

And then I got this great idea. Why not help my clients and audiences create a defining statement? Only I did not know how to do it nor knew what classified as a defining statement.

After careful thought and reflection, I created a set of rules and tips for creating a defining statement. If you hit 3 or 4 of the rules you will have a good one. If you hit 5, 6, or 7 of the rules, you will have a great one. Then the floodgates can open for you as they did for me and others around the country who have created a great defining statement.

Explanation of Rules

1 Language

Use eighth grade language. Don't assume your market is smart. It doesn't mean they are dumb. Too often we use complicated language and phrases that we don't even understand. Keep it simple.

2 Conversational

A defining statement is a simple answer to a simple question, "What do you do?" It is not an advertising theme, slogan, or tagline. If you will not say it, it is not a defining statement by my definition.

3 Attraction

It must attract people to you. Of course.

Note: It won't attract everyone, so don't get hung up on trying to create one that you think will.

4   Dream-focused

Focus on the dream of your prospects and the people you serve best. You will have a greater likelihood of attracting with the dreams versus pain-focused marketing efforts.

5   Contains What and Who

Identify the outcomes and who would be best served by working with you or buying from you.

6   Dual-focus

Create a two-part defining statement; i.e., two outcomes and you will appeal to a wider audience.

7   Repeatability

This may be the hardest rule to hit. If another person can repeat your defining statement or a part of it, then look out! Watch your referrals go way up!

Tips

- Use the words "work with"
- Use the word "want"
- Use one "and" in your statement
- Use three to five word outcomes

Tests

There are three tests you can take that will help you determine if your defining statement is a good one or a great one.

Test #1	Will I say it?
Test #2	Are others attracted to it?
Test #3	Could someone else say it?

How you answer these questions will determine if you have a good one or a great one. Don't settle for a good one. Keep going until you have a great one!

Speak and Float

When you create a great defining statement, you should be in a position to speak it and let it float in the marketplace. It takes a little courage and a little faith. But, those two things never hurt anyone.

The Traps

Often, people are fearful of limiting themselves in the marketplace. In reality, when you get a great defining statement, you will open yourself to more prospects and more opportunities.

Another trap is to create a defining statement and then put it on the shelf as if now that task is completed. Following are a number of ways you can use your defining statement.

"When a prospect calls
you and repeats your
defining statement
or a part of it
to you, you know
you have a great one!

Mark LeBlanc

Ways To Use A Defining Statement

1   Introduce yourself with it

2   Use it in your telemarketing efforts

3   Turn it into a headline for an ad/brochure

4   Use it on the homepage of your web site

5   Use it on your voice mail message

6   Put it on your fax cover sheet

7   Write articles built around it

8   Order promotional gifts or ad specialties
    with it printed on them

And the list goes on.

Note: When you get a great one, you are likely to look at it and think it is too simple. Sometimes your friends and family will think it is too simple. Bingo! You know you have a great one.

Final note: Great defining statements are so simple it is unlikely you could copyright or trademark them. It's okay. There's enough business to go around.

"Identify the issue,
listen for the other
person's mindset,
and respond in a way
which meets what that
person wants
and needs. If you
do, you will
create magic
with that person."

Mark LeBlanc

3

UNDERSTAND THE
MINDSET OF A PROSPECT

You will find that prospects fall into one of four mindsets when it comes to buying your products and engaging your services.

If you can identify the mindset of your prospect, and then respond in a manner that meets what that prospect wants and needs at that moment, you will go a long way toward building trust and rapport with your prospects. This is the ultimate communication tool, and it is so easy. It requires that you listen carefully. Before I share the four mindsets with you, I want you to understand two very important points.

1. This is not about good people and bad people.

2. Everyone falls between these mindsets, and you can move between the four in the blink of an eye. The four mindsets are:

   - A thinking mindset
   - A doing mindset
   - A struggling mindset
   - An achieving mindset

You can refer to people in these mindsets as Thinkers, Doers, Strugglers, and Achievers.

"A Thinker
is someone who
is thinking
about buying
your products
and services."

Mark LeBlanc

(not too hard, is it?)

The Thinker

A Thinker is someone who is thinking about buying your products and services. If you can understand this and respond accordingly, you can be of much better service.

Examples:

I am thinking about buying a car.
We've been thinking about remodeling our...
I think I will join a health club.
Maybe we should work with a financial planner.
I was wondering about...

And your Thinker flag goes up. If you know what this person wants and needs at this moment, you have it made.

WANT   to make a decision

NEED   information in order to make an informed decision

Do not try and sell to this prospect. Ask him or her how long they have been thinking about this? What kind of information are they looking for that would help them make this decision? What is their timeframe for making the decision? If you move quickly to sell this prospect, you run the risk of overwhelming him or her and thus alienating them.

"A Doer
is someone who
has made the
decision
to buy
your products
and services."

Mark LeBlanc

(get the picture?)

If you slow down and provide the information they need in order to make the best decision for them, you will earn their trust and respect.

The Doer

A Doer is someone who has made the decision to buy your products and services. And hopefully from you. If you understand this and respond accordingly, you will have a better chance of making the sale today.

Examples:

I've made the decision to buy a new car.
We're going to switch accounting firms.
I am going to lose 10 pounds in 90 days.
Let's find someone to manage our money.
I am going to start my business this summer.

And your Doer flag goes up. If you know what this person wants and needs at this moment, you have it made.

WANT   action

NEED   your sense of urgency

Move quickly with this prospect. Ask him or her how soon they would like to take possession, or get the ball rolling, or what their target date is.

Take charge of this sale. Keep an eye on being productive and don't waste time. You will delight your prospect, and you will stand head and shoulders above your competition.

"A Struggler
is someone who
is focused on
the costs
(time, energy, and/or money)
of
buying your
products and services."

Mark LeBlanc

The Struggler

A Struggler is someone who is in a momentary period of struggle. Everyone falls into this mindset from time to time depending on what issue or challenge is before us. If you can understand this prospect and respond accordingly, you can manage the sale properly or even let this one go. You don't have to sell everyone.

Examples:

You charge how much?
I'd never pay that price!
What kind of a deal can I get?
What is your hourly rate?
I am sooo busy. I just don't have time.

And your Struggler flag goes up. If you know what this person wants and needs at this moment, you have it made.

WANT   a quick fix

NEED   a new perspective

Be careful not to get wrapped up in this person's problems or you might find yourself in a moment of struggle. Draw this person out and help them think things through before they make a decision. You may need to provide a wake-up call or a new perspective. Don't make any mistakes and stick to your terms. If you bend the rules and go too far in order to accommodate this prospect, it will come back to haunt you.

"An Achiever
is someone who
is focused on
the outcomes
or what happens when
they use your
products or services."

Mark LeBlanc

The Achiever

Achievers are focused on what will happen when they put your products to good use or experience the results and benefits of your services. With most Achievers, what you charge is likely to be perceived as an investment in the outcomes provided rather than a cost for your products or services.

Listen for:

We're looking for someone we can work with.
I'd like to work with someone who will...
I'd rather pay a little more and make sure...
It's important we find someone we can trust.
Our suppliers are an important part of our team.

And your Achiever flag goes up! What a happy day! Make sure you respond accordingly.

WANT   teamwork

NEED   a resource

Here is your opportunity to build a relationship that can last. Find out what is most important to this person and how your competitors worked with him. See if you can uncover the pros and the cons of your competitors. An Achiever will give you a prescription to succeed or fail. Stay close, and never take this person for granted. If you do, you will lose, and they will look for another resource they can put on their team. That is a sad day.

Profile Of An Achiever

1

Achievers think things through
before they make a decision.

2

Once a decision is made, an
Achiever puts together a plan.

3

When problems surface, Achievers
look for creative ways of solving
these problems.

4

Achievers reach out for help
along the way. They know that
no one accomplishes anything
great, alone.

4

THE FOUR PHASES OF THE MARKETING AND SELLING PROCESS

There are four phases to the marketing and selling process. If you understand each phase and when you are in a specific phase, it will help you turn a prospect into a customer or let a prospect go when the fit is not right.

The Attraction Phase

The goal of the attraction phase is to get the ear of a prospect and generate interest in your products and services. It starts with creating a great defining statement and building all of your tools and materials around the outcomes of your work.

Then you can develop marketing, advertising, and promotional strategies that are consistent with the outcomes you determined. In the attraction phase, you are getting people to call you or to come to your place of business or to open your package.

Once there, you can move to the meaningful conversation or the meaningful copy that will sell a prospect on buying from you.

"Position
what prospects
need
in a way they
want
it, and you will
have people
busting your
door down."

Mark LeBlanc

The Meaningful Conversation Phase

The goal of the meaningful conversation phase is how you build your case in such a way that a prospect can make an informed decision.

A meaningful conversation can take a few minutes to an hour or more. In a complicated sale or transaction, it may require a series of meaningful conversations or interactions. The traditional book or course on selling included a section on uncovering a prospect's objections and having some fancy comeback or closing technique. Forget it. That process is tired, and today's prospects can smell these tactics. They're more likely to be irritated by them. Stick to the facts. And be able to articulate them.

Speak the truth about your company, your products, and your services. Then let the prospect make the decision that is best. When you build a better case for a prospect, then you can trust the decision of the prospect. If the answer is yes, it is the right answer. If the answer is no, that also is the right answer. This is referred to as honoring your prospects.

Following are three areas which make up the skeleton for a meaningful conversation. If you sprinkle in a few questions and respond appropriately, you will have a nice visit with a prospect, and your odds of getting a favorable result go up. You must be able to articulate the answers to these questions.

Area #1

How do you do what you do?

Area #2

Why should someone buy from you?

Area #3

What can a prospect really expect when they use your products and services?

Keep your answers to these questions simple and concise. In addition, here are several examples of questions you can add to round out your meaningful conversation.

Question #1

How long have you been thinking about buying this particular product or how long have you been in the market for these services?

Question #2

What is your timeframe for making your decision or how soon would you like to take delivery, etc.?

Question #3

How come you find yourself in this particular situation? Tell me a little more about...

Question #4

Are you presently talking with anyone else who provides these products and/or services?

These questions will help you pinpoint a prospect's needs and wants. In addition, you may uncover an obstacle or two that could get in the way of doing business. Better to find out sooner than later.

The Decision Phase

After you have built your case with a prospect, you have every right to ask two simple questions. I call these the courage questions.

1. Does this make sense?

2. Would you like to work with me?

or

Do you think this would be a good fit?

or

Would you like to receive a packet of info?

OSP versus ESP

Dr. Stanley Thomas in *Marketing To The Affluent*, briefly explains the difference between an ordinary salesperson (OSP) and an extraordinary salesperson (ESP).

An ESP has the courage to ask for the order or bring a sense of closure to the selling cycle.

An OSP lacks the necessary courage and can fall into the endless trap of being in the follow-up mode and never making a sale or the sales goal.

**From
The
Idea
File**

1. Track your meaningful conversations.

    _____   meaningful conversations without asking the courage questions

    _____   meaningful conversations with courage questions asked

If you are not reaching your optimistic number, it could be you are not having enough meaningful conversations.

The Engagement or Delivery Phase

The goal of the engagement phase is to communicate the scope of your work, your fees, your terms, and next steps for getting the ball rolling and getting the job done.

How often have you made a decision to buy a product or service and been frustrated by the person or the process a company has in place in order to do business with them? These companies have a weak engagement phase.

Your objective is to create a step-by-step process for working with your customers that takes the fear out of working with you, the surprise out of the invoice, and makes the decision an easy one for a prospect.

The Secret of Stimulating Referrals

Many people think referrals come from satisfied clients. Satisfied clients are usually just satisfied. The truth is most of our referrals come from our ecstatic or enthusiastic clients.

Here's a little secret for you. You can turn a satisfied client into an ecstatic client if that person enjoyed the process of working with you. If you create a way of doing business; i.e., through your engagement phase, which is enjoyable, then watch your referrals double, triple, and quadruple!

Find a Blend

Many of us are in different small businesses and sell a variety of products and services. Take these issues and questions and apply them to your unique situation. You may add one or two to your current selling strategies or look at revamping your selling process.

Look for the common threads. After looking at what has worked for you in the past, mix in some of the ideas in this book.

5

DEVELOP A M.A.P. ATTACK
MARKETING, ADVERTISING, PROMOTION

The world is full of marketing experts and books on marketing strategies and tactics. Let's step back and reframe this in a way that makes sense, and you can figure out what will work for you.

There is only one goal. And that goal is to get your phone to ring and to get a prospect to walk in your door. Simple ideas when put into action on a consistent basis will produce better results than any one shot marketing or advertising blitz.

People invest thousands of dollars every year and every day to "put out" a great mailing or create a fancy web site. They believe this will be the answer to their prayers. Take that same money and divide it by twelve.

Now step back and look for creative ways to use that money on an ongoing basis. I would guess that you have many marketing books on your shelf outlining dozens of strategies that will work. They will work if you take action, put them in place, and do them over and over again.

The Magic Is In The Mix

Promoting your business is something you must do on a daily basis. Some things should work for you automatically or while you sleep. Other things you should be taking action on monthly and weekly.

The seeds you plant today will reap a huge harvest tomorrow. If you market or promote yourself on an inconsistent basis, then your revenues are likely to ride that roller coaster.

[Important note: Without knowing who you are and what you do, it is difficult for me to know what quantities or frequency is doable for you. While I can throw out some examples, it really is up to you. How much is enough? or How will I know if I am doing the right things? Look at your deposit book. Are you at or near your optimistic number on a regular basis?]

Following are examples of consistent marketing strategies you may consider in your business or professional practice.

1. Direct Mail

   Send 1,000 or 500 or 100 pieces of direct mail every month.

2. Telemarketing

   Call 500 or 250 or 100 prospects every week or every month.

3. Networking

   Attend four or two or one networking opportunity every single month.

4. Trade Shows

   Exhibit at a trade show quarterly or twice or even once a year.

5. Advertising

   Place a small display ad or even a well-written classified ad in a targeted publication every week or month of the year.

6. Speak

   Never turn down an opportunity to share a message with a civic, trade, or professional group. Join Toastmasters International.

7. Newsletters

   Start a quarterly or monthly newsletter and mail to your database of prospects and customers. Consider an e-mail newsletter.

8. Internet

   Create a web site. This can be as simple or as interactive as you like and what will work for you.

   Enlist the help of an internet professional. The right one can make a big difference in the development and effectiveness of your site. Get to know the search engine process.

9. Contribute

   If you are going to make a donation or contribution, make a big one. Invest time, energy, as well as money. Have some fun with it! Get behind a cause.

You may have other ongoing strategies in place or under consideration. On purpose, I stayed away from radio, television, and billboards. If these are possible for you and can work for you, go for it. They tend to be cost prohibitive for the micro and small business owner to consider.

Here are some other ideas that will support your marketing efforts and help you create an identity in the marketplace.

 From The Idea File

Examples of marketing ideas

1. Get a great company name.

   Never underestimate the importance of a company name. How does it help your marketing efforts? Consider upgrading your company name if it will do a better job of positioning your company in the marketplace.

2. Turn your fax cover sheet into a billboard.

3. Change your voicemail frequently.

   Put a marketing message on your outgoing message. Say thank you!

4. Have a giveaway.

   Find something for a dollar or a quarter or a dime and buy thousands of them with your name and number on them.

5. Find a marketing partner.

   Find an ally or cooperative business partner and look for ways to cross promote each other.

6. Send a holiday card.

   Consider sending a holiday card right before Thanksgiving rather than at Christmas time. Spend a little extra money and make it the first one they will receive, and the nicest.

7. Time your database mailings.

   If you want to spend money on a mailing to your database, then have it hit their mailbox the day after Labor Day and/or the first working day of the new year.

   These two days are natural days of renewal. Hit 'em when they're getting back to work!

8. Get the right tools in place.

   If you are trying to "do it all" with one telephone line or one piece of equipment, forget it. The message you are sending is "You don't care enough about me to put the right tools in place." It is a moment of irritation for your prospects and customers.

   Example: Having to turn on your computer to receive a fax, because you are too cheap to have a dedicated line for faxing and on-line applications.

9. Create a set of promotional materials you can fax or e-mail to a prospect.

   In addition to having a brochure or pro-motional package, have a set of materials you can fax or e-mail right after a mean-ingful conversation with a prospect on the telephone.

10. Keep your written letters or memos ASAP (As Short As Possible.)

There are five ways you can communicate or connect with your advocates.

The Greatest Marketing Strategy In The World

Here is an ongoing marketing strategy you can put in place and get great results. It is simple, your investment is quite low, and the return can be high. I know of no other strategy that costs so little and produces so much.

The objective is to create an advocate system in the marketplace. I first got a hint of this in '83 when I heard a friend and colleague, Dr. Lyman K. (Manny) Steil, CSP, CPAE conduct a presentation on how to listen more effectively.

He described an exercise that consisted of identifying the 25 people in your life that you most need to listen to and be in a relationship with. Later, I expanded the idea and created a different version of the Target 25 strategy.

Target 25

Start by making a list of the 25 most important people in your life who are in a position to impact your business.

Two Key Points

- Never let an advocate get more than thirty days away from you.

- He or she must know your defining statement.

Note: If your defining statement is repeatable, and you put it in the back pocket of an advocate, watch your referrals go up!

Communicate

There are five ways you can communicate with your advocate group. Or should I say connect? If these people are truly your advocates in the marketplace, then it is your responsibility to stay connected with them. You can communicate or connect by phone, fax, mail, e-mail, and personal visit.

Your Investment

Your Target 25 strategy should cost you between zero and $50 dollars per month on average. Your investment of time should average one to four hours per month. If you are spending more money or it's taking more time, you may be making this too complicated.

Evaluation

Periodically, you should re-evaluate your group of advocates, add new ones, and wean off those people who are really supporters. Make an effort to stay connected with your supporters on a different basis.

People ask, "If twenty-five is good, would fifty be better?" The answer is no. It will not be possible to stay connected on a regular basis if your advocate group becomes just another database and gets larger and larger.

Annual Plan

Put together a list of 12 things you can do over the next 12 months to stay connected with your advocates. Be creative and yet, keep it simple, so you will not miss a month.

Examples:

1. call them
2. send them your bio and card
3. ad specialty
4. write/find an article and send copies
5. postcard
6. e-mail a quick note
7. face-to-face visit once a year
8. fax a note
9. holiday card or gift
10. newsletter
11. call again
12. repeat any of the above

Keep it simple and be gracious. It goes way beyond any referrals you might get from an advocate. The friendship and support are invaluable. Being in business for yourself is not easy. The bonus with this strategy is that it is awfully hard to get down in the dumps for very long when you realize you have a small army of advocates who truly care about you.

Your advocates will go out of their way to say good things about you and initiate some type of connection on your behalf. Some of them will use this powerful phrase:

"Got to"

You have *got to* call Bill or Suzie and find out about their products and services. Soon you will get calls from people who literally will say, "I don't know who you are, but so and so said I had to call you. What do you do?"

"Focus
on what you
can
realistically
do on a
regular
basis in order to
reach
your optimistic
number."

Mark LeBlanc

6

KEEP YOUR FOCUS
ON A DAILY BASIS

Focusing may be one of the hardest things you will do in your business. Staying focused and on track is nearly impossible.

Many of you talk a good game. The reality is, we are human. That same freedom we crave as business owners and entrepreneurs can also be our downfall.

When you are working 40 to 50 to 60 hours a week for someone else, you would never think to stay home and do the laundry or take a nap. Or even feel that you are entitled to do that.

Funny, how you can start a business and part of your brain goes right out of your ears. Long lunches, picking up the kids from school, a soap opera, mowing the lawn, reading the paper, and a computer game take on new significance. Here is a way you can solve this challenge of staying focused and on track.

Create a set of activities that you can do on a regular basis. Keep adjusting until you have the right activities that have a greater likelihood of you reaching your optimistic number.

This is an important part of creating a model that drives you and that you can be excited about. I refer to these activities as benchmarks you can set up and measure on a monthly basis. You can take any objective and create a set or series of benchmarks that will move you forward.

You can create a set of financial benchmarks, marketing benchmarks, selling benchmarks, and yes, even fun benchmarks.

The following benchmarks are examples in order to get you thinking. These benchmarks are monthly benchmarks. Create your own set. If some of the following will work for you, you may need to increase or decrease the amounts or frequencies. Examples:

Financial

Monthly revenues (optimistic number)
Invest $250 for retirement
Donate $100 to favorite charity
Owner's compensation ??????

Marketing

2 networking meetings
Target 25 (yes/no)
Send 200 pieces of direct mail
Make 100 telemarketing calls

Selling

8 new clients
30 meaningful conversations
$5,000 in product sales
Spend 4 hours on skills training

Fun

One 3-day weekend away from work
Read 1 non-business book
4 family/date/friend nights
Go dancing twice a month

This may seem elementary. Something magical happens when you commit your thoughts, ideas, dreams, goals, and intentions to paper.

The people who understand have done it, and witnessed firsthand the results of what happens when you get something out of your head and in front of you on paper. If you have never done it, try it. Something great will happen.

 From The Idea File

1. Create one benchmark for each of the following four areas:

Financial: _____

                      _____

Marketing: _____

                      _____

Selling: _____

                      _____

Fun: _____

                      _____

The RRR Philosophy

Focus on what you can *realistically* do on a *regular* basis in order to *reach* your optimistic number. Otherwise, you might fall into one of two traps.

Trap #1   The Great Commitment

The great commitment is an example of those moments when we get sick and tired of an issue or situation, and we firmly resolve that this time it is going to change. These commitments or resolutions are usually broken in a short period of time.

Trap #2   The Great Compromise

The great compromise is where most of us live, work, and play. It's an attitude that permeates our society. Remember when you graduated from high school or the time you set out to conquer the world and make your mark in this life? What happened to that person? Some day never happens when you live and love in the land of compromise. What does this have to do with business? Everything.

Let's get your enthusiasm back.

I can think of no other way to build momentum than to create a set of activities that is doable on a monthly, weekly, and/or daily basis.

Example: I walk a mile a day.

              Why? Because I can.

It will create a foundation for higher achievement you will find unstoppable. The only thing you have control of is how you think, take action, and live on a daily basis.

The "Simple"

Give "The Simple" everything you've got. It won't be easy. And when it seems as if no one understands the challenges and struggle of being in business; know that many others have come and gone before you. Thousands are experiencing the joy of going it alone. Reach out for help. You will accomplish more when you reach out for help than if you hang on to your stubbornness and think you can figure it out all by yourself. It takes two!

If you have your eye on the big picture, focus on the month at hand, if you craft a model that drives you, if you position yourself properly, if you serve others in a way that meets what they want and need, if you surround yourself with people who really care about your success, if you are willing to track and measure your progress on a regular basis...

Anything is possible!

It takes two!

The following 10 books have had the most impact and influence on my life and work.

1. *The Greatest Salesman In The World*
2. *The Greatest Miracle In The World*
   both by Og Mandino

3. *Selling The Dream*
   by Guy Kawasaki

4. *The Power of Purpose*
   by Richard J. Lieder

5. *The Eagle's Secret*
   by David McNally

6. *Tuesdays With Morrie*
   by Mitch Albom

7. *Wealth In A Decade*
   by Brett Machtig

8. *Work In Progress*
   by Michael Eisner

9. *People Of The Lie*
   by Scott M. Peck

10. *It's So Cold In Minnesota!*
    by Cathy McGlynn* and Bonnie Stewart

* Cathy (LeBlanc) McGlynn is my sister. On a frigid, January day in Minnesota, she and Bonnie Stewart took a silly idea and put it in print. It has become a holiday best seller in Minnesota! I am so proud of her! It is a classic example of how a person can experience success when he or she takes action on an idea.

"Mark LeBlanc is an original and may be one of the great influencers of the coming century."

Nina Woolverton
Signature Speakers

Presentation Information

Growing Your Business!

Mark conducts his flagship presentation for groups of small business owners who want to grow their business and with professionals who want to sell more of their products and services. Depending on your format, time available, and meeting objectives, his presentation can run from thirty minutes to three days. It zeros in on the core issues which owners face on a daily basis...more focus, more prospects, more referrals, and ultimately more business!

For availability and booking information, call your favorite speakers bureau or you can reach Mark direct at 800-690-0810.

Final Thoughts

1. Share **Growing Your Business!** with your friends, family members, and colleagues. Check out your local bookstore or order it online through Amazon.com or other online booksellers. For volume discounts, contact Uncle Miltie at Beaver's Pond Press.

2. **Send us your comments.** We'd like to hear your success stories, insights, and any ideas you have for our future reference and additional books. Mail or send an e-mail to:

    Small Business Success
    7825 Fay Avenue, Suite 200
    La Jolla, CA 92037

    mleblanc@san.rr.com

3. **Check out www.tailwind.com**. It is a great place for information, ideas, services, and products for business owners on the grow.

4. **It Takes Two!** Thank you to all of my friends, my family, my book team, my clients, and my colleagues in Master Speakers International and the National Speakers Association. Your faith in me and support of my work has surpassed my wildest dreams.

Mark LeBlanc
October, 1999